"This series is a tremendous resource for those wanting to study and teach the Bible with an understanding of how the gospel is woven throughout Scripture. Here are gospel-minded pastors and scholars doing gospel business from all the Scriptures. This is a biblical and theological feast preparing God's people to apply the entire Bible to all of life with heart and mind wholly committed to Christ's priorities."

BRYAN CHAPELL, President Emeritus, Covenant Theological Seminary; Senior Pastor, Grace Presbyterian Church, Peoria, Illinois

"Mark Twain may have smiled when he wrote to a friend, 'I didn't have time to write you a short letter, so I wrote you a long letter.' But the truth of Twain's remark remains serious and universal, because well-reasoned, compact writing requires extra time and extra hard work. And this is what we have in the Crossway Bible study series *Knowing the Bible*. The skilled authors and notable editors provide the contours of each book of the Bible as well as the grand theological themes that bind them together as one Book. Here, in a 12-week format, are carefully wrought studies that will ignite the mind and the heart."

R. KENT HUGHES, Visiting Professor of Practical Theology, Westminster Theological Seminary

"*Knowing the Bible* brings together a gifted team of Bible teachers to produce a high-quality series of study guides. The coordinated focus of these materials is unique: biblical content, provocative questions, systematic theology, practical application, and the gospel story of God's grace presented all the way through Scripture."

PHILIP G. RYKEN, President, Wheaton College

"These *Knowing the Bible* volumes provide a significant and very welcome variation on the general run of inductive Bible studies. This series provides substantial instruction, as well as teaching through the very questions that are asked. *Knowing the Bible* then goes even further by showing how any given text links with the gospel, the whole Bible, and the formation of theology. I heartily endorse this orientation of individual books to the whole Bible and the gospel, and I applaud the demonstration that sound theology was not something invented later by Christians, but is right there in the pages of Scripture."

GRAEME L. GOLDSWORTHY, former lecturer, Moore Theological College; author, *According to Plan*, *Gospel and Kingdom*, *The Gospel in Revelation*, and *Gospel and Wisdom*

"What a gift to earnest, Bible-loving, Bible-searching believers! The organization and structure of the Bible study format presented through the *Knowing the Bible* series is so well conceived. Students of the Word are led to understand the content of passages through perceptive, guided questions, and they are given rich insights and application all along the way in the brief but illuminating sections that conclude each study. What potential growth in depth and breadth of understanding these studies offer! One can only pray that vast numbers of believers will discover more of God and the beauty of his Word through these rich studies."

BRUCE A. WARE, Professor of Christian Theology, The Southern Baptist Theological Seminary

KNOWING THE BIBLE

J. I. Packer, Theological Editor
Dane C. Ortlund, Series Editor
Lane T. Dennis, Executive Editor

• • • • • •

Genesis
Exodus
Leviticus
Deuteronomy
Joshua
Ruth and Esther
1–2 Kings
Ezra and Nehemiah
Job
Psalms
Proverbs
Ecclesiastes
Isaiah
Jeremiah
Daniel
Hosea
Matthew
Mark
Luke
John
Acts
Romans
1 Corinthians
2 Corinthians
Galatians
Ephesians
Philippians
Colossians and Philemon
1–2 Thessalonians
1–2 Timothy and Titus
Hebrews
James
1–2 Peter and Jude
Revelation

• • • • • •

J. I. PACKER is Board of Governors' Professor of Theology at Regent College (Vancouver, BC). Dr. Packer earned his DPhil at the University of Oxford. He is known and loved worldwide as the author of the best-selling book *Knowing God*, as well as many other titles on theology and the Christian life. He serves as the General Editor of the ESV Bible and as the Theological Editor for the *ESV Study Bible*.

LANE T. DENNIS is President of Crossway, a not-for-profit publishing ministry. Dr. Dennis earned his PhD from Northwestern University. He is Chair of the ESV Bible Translation Oversight Committee and Executive Editor of the *ESV Study Bible*.

DANE C. ORTLUND is Executive Vice President of Bible Publishing and Bible Publisher at Crossway. He is a graduate of Covenant Theological Seminary (MDiv, ThM) and Wheaton College (BA, PhD). Dr. Ortlund has authored several books and scholarly articles in the areas of Bible, theology, and Christian living.

JOB

A 12-WEEK STUDY

Eric Ortlund

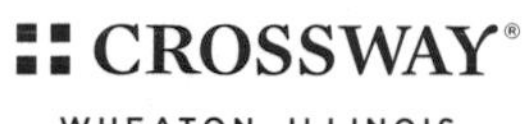

WHEATON, ILLINOIS

Knowing the Bible: Job, A 12-Week Study

Published by Crossway
1300 Crescent Street
Wheaton, Illinois 60187

Cover design: Simplicated Studio

First printing 2017

Printed in the United States of America

All emphases in Scripture quotations have been added by the author.

Trade paperback ISBN: 978-1–4335-5104-8
EPub ISBN: 978-1–4335-5107-9
PDF ISBN: 978-1–4335-5105-5
Mobipocket ISBN: 978-1–4335-5106-2

Crossway is a publishing ministry of Good News Publishers.

VP 28 27 26 25 24 23 22 21 20 19 18 17
15 14 13 12 11 10 9 8 7 6 5 4 3 2 1

TABLE OF CONTENTS

SERIES PREFACE

KNOWING THE BIBLE, as the series title indicates, was created to help readers know and understand the meaning, the message, and the God of the Bible. Each volume in the series consists of 12 units that progressively take the reader through a clear, concise study of that book of the Bible. In this way, any given volume can fruitfully be used in a 12-week format either in group study, such as in a church-based context, or in individual study. Of course, these 12 studies could be completed in fewer or more than 12 weeks, as convenient, depending on the context in which they are used.

Each study unit gives an overview of the text at hand before digging into it with a series of questions for reflection or discussion. The unit then concludes by highlighting the gospel of grace in each passage ("Gospel Glimpses"), identifying whole-Bible themes that occur in the passage ("Whole-Bible Connections"), and pinpointing Christian doctrines that are affirmed in the passage ("Theological Soundings").

The final component to each unit is a section for reflecting on personal and practical implications from the passage at hand. The layout provides space for recording responses to the questions proposed, and we think readers need to do this to get the full benefit of the exercise. The series also includes definitions of key words. These definitions are indicated by a note number in the text and are found at the end of each chapter.

Lastly, to help understand the Bible in this deeper way, we urge readers to use the ESV Bible and the *ESV Study Bible*, which are available in various print and digital formats, including online editions at esv.org. The Knowing the Bible series is also available online. Additional 12-week studies covering each book of the Bible will be added as they become available.

May the Lord greatly bless your study as you seek to know him through knowing his Word.

J. I. Packer
Lane T. Dennis

Week 1: Overview

Getting Acquainted

The book of Job narrates the agony and faith of a great saint in order to teach us about the way in which the Lord governs his world, and how we can trust him when we suffer. Job was a deeply spiritual man who was greatly blessed for his faith (see Job 1:1–3), but when the motives for Job's piety were questioned by the Accuser, the Lord allowed Job to lose every earthly blessing in order to prove the genuineness of his dependence upon God. Job's friends visited him with good intentions (2:11; 33:32) but only caused him more pain (19:12) by insisting that he must have sinned in order to have provoked such brutal treatment from God. Job admits he has needed forgiveness many times but insists he has walked in integrity with God and has done nothing to deserve such suffering. As a result, Job finds himself forced to the terrifying but mistaken conclusion that God has treated him unjustly—that God is not fully just or good or trustworthy. Even while saying these dark things about God, however, Job will also express remarkable faith and a certainty that he will be reconciled to the Lord.

The debate between Job and his friends over the character of God and Job and, by extension, over the moral order of life only alienates and embitters Job. It is not until the Lord himself speaks to Job about the way in which he rules the universe—and what place he allows for evil—that Job is comforted. Having proved that he loves God for God's sake, irrespective of any blessing God might grant, Job is restored to the full and blessed life that God desires for all of his children. (For further background, see the *ESV Study Bible*, pages 869–873; available online at esv.org.)

Placing Job in the Larger Story

The Old Testament has much to say about suffering and interprets it in various ways. In Deuteronomy, God warns that his destructive curse will fall on Israel if they break covenant with him and trust in other gods (Deuteronomy 28). Proverbs often states that sin brings about suffering as its natural consequence (e.g., Prov. 10:14). In the book of Job, on the other hand, the title character suffers *precisely because he is so devout*—and he suffers in a way that is unbearable and impossible for him to explain. The book of Job thus nuances and deepens how we are to think about suffering and about why God sometimes allows pain that seems to serve no purpose and have no explanation. The book shows us how to speak to extreme suffering and demonstrates the promises God makes to us in our suffering.

As we will see, Job prefigures Jesus in that both men suffer greatly because of their obedience to God in order to further God's purposes, to defeat the accusations of the Accuser, and to glorify the Lord.

Key Verse

"Does Job fear God for no reason?" (Job 1:9)

Date and Historical Background

Job lived outside of Israel: the "land of Uz" (Job 1:1) is either close to Edom or is another name for that country (see Lam. 4:21; Jer. 25:20). There are a variety of indications in the book that Job lived in the earliest stages of Old Testament history. For example, Ezekiel refers to Job as a well-known figure of remarkable piety (Ezek. 14:14). Further, Job and his friends refer to God most often with the archaic name *Shaddai* (see Ex. 6:3). They know some truths about God but never refer to the covenants between the Lord and Israel. Job also lives to a very old age (140 years; 42:16) and sacrifices without a priest, as Abraham did (Job 1:5). For these and other reasons, this story seems to take place around the time of the early chapters of Genesis.

The narrator of the story, however, refers in chapters 1–2 and in the Lord's speeches in chapters 38–41 to the covenant name *Yahweh*—the name by which God revealed himself to Israel (Ex. 3:12–14). Although the narrator does not identify himself, the fact that he narrates events that transpire in heaven, of which the human characters of the book are not aware, suggests that an inspired Israelite has shaped a story about a famous man in order to teach us about God's providence and loyalty to him in suffering. We do not know in which period of Israelite history this narrator lived.

Outline

I. Job's Tragedy (1:1–2:13)

II. Job's Cosmic Lament over His Suffering (3:1–26)

III. The Debate between Job and His Friends over the Meaning of His Suffering (4:1–31:40)

   A. Round one (4:1–14:22)

      1. Eliphaz (4:1–5:27)
      2. Job (6:1–7:21)
      3. Bildad (8:1–22)
      4. Job (9:1–10:22)
      5. Zophar (11:1–20)
      6. Job (12:1–14:22)

   B. Round two (15:1–21:34)

      1. Eliphaz (15:1–35)
      2. Job (16:1–17:16)
      3. Bildad (18:1–21)
      4. Job (19:1–29)
      5. Zophar (20:1–29)
      6. Job (21:1–34)

   C. Round three (22:1–27:23)

      1. Eliphaz (22:1–30)
      2. Job (23:1–24:25)
      3. Bildad (25:1–6)
      4. Job (26:1–27:23)

   D. Interlude: Where can wisdom be found? (28:1–28)

   E. Job's final defense (29:1–31:40)

IV. Elihu's Speeches (32:1–37:24)

V. The Lord's Speeches (38:1–41:34)

   A. First speech: Creation and its inhabitants (38:1–40:5)

      1. The architecture of creation (38:1–38)
      2. Different animals in creation (38:39–39:30)
      3. Job's first response (40:1–5)

   B. Second speech: Behemoth and Leviathan (40:6–41:34)

      1. The preparation of the divine warrior (40:6–14)
      2. Behemoth (40:15–24)
      3. Leviathan (41:1–34)

VI. Job's Restoration (42:1–17)

   A. Job's second response and his spiritual restoration (42:1–6)

   B. Job's social and physical restoration (42:7–17)

As You Get Started

What is your understanding of how the book of Job contributes to the Bible? What do we learn of in this book that no other book teaches us?

it is an Old Testament parable

God's use of suffering to further his purpose

What is your current understanding of what the book of Job contributes to Christian theology? What does this book teach us about God, his character and action, and how we are to respond to him?

it illustrates that while our sins are forgiven, we can still have the consequences in our lives of sin

He never changes, every thing he does is part of his plan for us and we should thank and praise him in every circumstance

Job is perhaps the most difficult Bible book to understand. What questions do you have about it? What confuses you? What would you like to have clarified by the end of this study?

What role does Job's wife play - why is she not as pious as Job -

As You Finish This Unit . . .

Take a few minutes to ask God to bless you with increased understanding and a transformed heart and life as you begin this study of Job.

Week 2: Job's Tragedy

Job 1:1–2:13

The Place of the Passage

The first section of Job introduces the issue that drives the entire book: why did God allow such horrifying suffering to befall someone who was so loyal to him, who seemed to "deserve" so much better? In these brief chapters, we learn of God's sovereignty over everything in creation, and we gain insight into a great contest that is being fought in heaven over the saints. We see how much God cares for his own glory and for the purity of our relationship with him. And we see a great saint suffer greatly, yet worship in the most costly, beautiful way possible.

The Big Picture

Job 1–2 reveals a dramatic struggle in heaven over the saints and, by extension, over the glory of God. The great question driving these chapters is whether Job will persevere in faith in God when it costs him every earthly blessing.

Reflection and Discussion

Read through the complete passage for this study, Job 1:1–2:13. Then review the questions below concerning this introductory section to Job's story and write your notes on them. (For further background, see the *ESV Study Bible*, pages 874–876; available online at esv.org.)

1. Job's First Test (1:1–22)

The first five verses of Job 1 show us Job's wonderfully blessed life. In verses 1–3, what aspect of Job's life is described first, and why is it important that we are told of this before anything else? What do we learn about Job's family life and his deepest concerns for his family in verses 4–5?

Job was richly blessed in his relationship with the Lord. What blessings do you enjoy in your relationship with God, even if they are not identical to Job's?

In verses 6–12, the scene shifts to the throne room of heaven. Although ancient Israelites might not have known everything that the New Testament reveals about Satan,[1] what do we learn about him, his intentions and plans, and his relationship to God? What do we learn about God's sovereignty?

Satan's question in 1:9, "Does Job fear God[2] for no reason?," is most significant. What is Satan implying about Job's motives and the basis of his relationship with God? If Satan is right, how should God treat Job? Why might it be important for God to allow a terrible test of Job's devotion to him?

Like clockwork, in 1:13–19 Job loses every secondary blessing that was listed in 1:2–3. Some elements of Job's tragedy have naturalistic causes (e.g., the Sabeans in v. 15), while some are supernatural (the fire from heaven in v. 16). We know that Satan is the one at work behind the scenes, but what would Job have concluded about the cause of these losses? (In the worldview of Job's day, such events were interpreted not as random tragedies but as signs of divine wrath.)

Job's response to his losses is as poignant as it is noble (1:20–21). How does he express his grief as well as his devotion to God? How does his worship prove that Satan's claim in 1:9 was false? How does Job's worship guide our own in instances when God allows some great or tragic loss?

2. Job's Second Test (2:1–13)

The Lord's statement in 2:3 that Satan "incited" him against Job "without reason" is clear at one level—the Lord is acknowledging that the test was needless and that Job did not deserve this treatment. But this statement can also be troubling, since it might appear that God is admitting that he was tricked or manipulated. But how do we see God continuing to defend his servant against Satan? And does the echoing phrase "for no reason" (1:9) and "without reason" (2:3) imply a deeper reason behind God's actions?

Satan responds to the Lord by implying that Job's first test was not deep enough. What is Satan's second proposal, and why does he think this will break Job's devotion to God?

Reflect on the short speech of Job's wife in 2:9. Would she have passed Satan's test in 1:9? What do we learn about the quality of Job's loyalty to God from his response to his wife (v. 10)?

Job's three friends arrive in 2:11. What is their motive in traveling to see Job? What does their shock and grief imply about their expectations for what they would find? What might we expect the friends to say to Job in the following chapters, given their intentions?

Read through the following three sections on *Gospel Glimpses*, *Whole-Bible Connections*, and *Theological Soundings*. Then take time to consider the *Personal Implications* these sections may have for you.

Gospel Glimpses

GOD'S GRACE. Job lives out his faith in beautiful and costly ways (see 29:11–17), but when God takes from him his family and wealth, Job speaks only of what God had *given* him (1:21). Job considers his deeply blessed life a gift, not something he was owed in return for his good behavior. When he loses everything, he is not angry with God for betraying him but worships God just as sincerely as when he enjoyed all of his blessings. Job's relationship with God is clearly based on grace, not reward or merit. What Job loves most deeply in life is his deep friendship with God (see 29:4); for him, everything else is a gift. We also see God's grace in his enthusiastic recommendation of Job. Although Job was a sinner (see 31:33–34), God had only positive things to say about "his servant," a term that puts Job in the exalted company of Abraham (Gen. 26:24), Moses (Ex. 14:31), and David (2 Sam. 7:5). As we will see, everyone will turn on Job except God. No one defends him as enthusiastically as God does, all on terms of grace, not merit.

CHRIST PREFIGURED. Job is not an "everyman." Of how many of us would God say, "There is none like him on the earth" (Job 1:8)? And even though God does allow Job-like suffering in our lives, none of us will suffer in so extreme and total a way as Job did. In both Job's deep piety and his suffering, he prefigures that greater man, Jesus Christ, who innocently suffers the wrath of God in order to refute the accusations of the Devil and to glorify God.

Whole-Bible Connections

RETRIBUTION AND REWARD. Both Testaments clearly teach that faithful obedience to God, even when imperfect, is rewarded with blessing even in this life (Eliphaz neatly defines it in 4:7–8; see also Mark 10:29–30; Gal. 6:7). The book of Job does not contradict this teaching, because Job finishes the book twice as blessed as he was before (Job 42:10). But Job will nuance our understanding of the doctrine of retribution: sometimes God interrupts his normal policy of blessing our obedience in order to allow the kind of suffering we would expect to fall on someone openly defiant of God and hurtful toward others. Although the book of Job teaches us that these experiences are temporary, it also insists that God sometimes allows them in order to seal us in our relationship with him.

DIFFERENT KINDS OF SUFFERING. Suffering is diagnosed in different ways in the Bible: sometimes, it is the direct result of sin (see Ps. 38:3–5); at other times, God allows pain in order for us to mature as Christians (see Rom. 5:3–5). But neither of these explanations is applicable to Job. The first two chapters of Job go out of their way to show that it is for no sin in Job's life that he is suffering—not even Satan can find fault with him! Furthermore, God is not trying to grow Job spiritually. Job is already a mature saint—and if Job did receive some spiritual virtue from his ordeal, Satan could have repeated his accusation that Job loved God only for the secondary benefits, this time pointing to spiritual benefits instead of material ones. The book of Job teaches that saints who imperfectly but sincerely serve God will sometimes suffer for no reason they can explain in relation to past sin, and will perhaps not seem to grow spiritually from the ordeal. Job's suffering is of a kind that will lead only to a deeper vision of God himself (Job 42:5).

Theological Soundings

THE GLORY OF GOD AND THE TESTING OF THE SAINTS. "Does Job fear God for no reason?" (Job 1:9) is a question that should make every Christian nervous. It is easy to drift unconsciously from honoring the Lord as our only real treasure and great joy, to viewing him as a business partner or Santa Claus. This is clearly not true for Job: Job loves and fears God for God's sake alone, irrespective of what secondary blessings Job gains or loses in the relationship. But do we? It is beneficial to use Job's worship in 1:5 as a guide for our own when we are in good health, surrounded by our family. But would we be just as enthusiastic in worship if we were at death's door or had lost a child in a car accident? If God loves us, he will at some point put us in a position where we must worship him for his own sake, in the midst of agony. The book of Job teaches us that God must sometimes allow this kind of suffering if he is going to save us, because a relationship with God for God's sake, not merely viewing him as a dispenser of blessing, is the only kind of relationship that will save us. If we love God only for what he gives us in this life and not for himself, we are serving ourselves, not him. When God allows Job-like suffering in our lives, his greater purpose is to deliver us from our trivializing of him.

GOD'S SOVEREIGNTY. The book of Job gives us a nuanced understanding of God's rule over all things. Sometimes Christians speak of God as the sole immediate cause behind every occurrence in their lives, but Job shows that other hostile forces are sometimes also at work when we suffer. At the same time, it is clear that Satan can attack Job's family, property, and health only with God's permission and within the boundaries God has set (1:12; 2:6). Furthermore, when God finally speaks to Job, he does not shift the blame for Job's suffering to Satan. Although the Lord is not the direct cause behind Job's suffering, he is ultimately responsible for it (see 42:11). This helps us understand the complex nature of God's rule. Regardless of what we as believers might suffer, we are always in the hands of a loving God.

Personal Implications

Take time to reflect on the implications of Job 1–2 for your own life today. Consider what you have learned that might lead you to praise God, repent of sin, and trust in his gracious promises. Make notes below on the personal implications for your walk with the Lord of the (1) *Gospel Glimpses*, (2) *Whole-Bible Connections*, (3) *Theological Soundings*, and (4) this passage as a whole.

1. Gospel Glimpses

2. Whole-Bible Connections

3. Theological Soundings

4. Job 1–2

As You Finish This Unit . . .

Take a moment now to ask for the Lord's blessing and help as you continue in this study of Job. And take a moment also to look back through this unit of study, to reflect on some key things that the Lord may be teaching you—and perhaps to highlight and underline these things to review again in the future.

Definitions

[1] **Satan** – A spiritual being whose name means "accuser." As the leader of all the demonic forces, he opposes God's rule and seeks to harm God's people and accuse them of wrongdoing. His power, however, is confined to the bounds that God has set for him, and one day he will be destroyed along with all his demons (Matt. 25:41; Rev. 20:10).

[2] **The fear of the Lord** – A godly, wise fear that demonstrates awe and reverence for the all-powerful God (Prov. 1:7).

Week 3: Job's Cosmic Lament

Job 3:1–26

The Place of the Passage

Job has lost everything in a series of quick tragedies, and his friends have now arrived. It is Job, however, who speaks first, and his first speech sets in motion the long debate in the book of Job. From Job's perspective, God has turned on him in a series of angry judgments—God has started to treat Job as if he were a grave sinner. Although Job knows he has done nothing to deserve God's curse, he finds himself forced into the terrifying position of wondering if it would have been better if he had never been born.

The Big Picture

In Job 3, we see a vision of despair as Job contemplates life without a relationship with God.

Reflection and Discussion

Read through the entire text for this study, Job 3. Then interact with the following questions concerning this section of Job and record your notes on them. (For further background, see the *ESV Study Bible*, pages 876–878; available online at esv.org.)

1. A Curse on Job's "Day" and "Night" (3:1–10)

In 3:1–3, Job wishes that the day on which he was born would "perish"—that it would be, as it were, forever erased from God's heavenly calendar. Although Job is in incredible pain, this wish appears to be something of an overreaction: it would make sense for Job to wish he was no longer alive, but why would he wish he had never been born in the first place? From Job's perspective, God is (inexplicably) angry with him and is treating him like a sinner. What does it say about how Job values God that, suffering under what appears to be God's disapproval, he wishes he had never lived at all?

In 3:4–10, Job alternates between the themes of day and night, forming a chiastic[1] pattern. Although it is probably clearer in the original Hebrew, Job's curse of the day of his birth echoes Genesis 1 in a number of ways; for instance, Job's first statement in verse 4—"Let that day be darkness!"—reverses God's beginning declaration in Genesis 1:3, "Let there be light!" Take some time to let these images sink in. What vision of the universe is being described? As you look at life and all of God's creation through Job's eyes, what do you see?

The verb translated in verse 5 as "claim" is the same word used for God's wonderful acts of salvation on Israel's behalf elsewhere in the Old Testament, often translated "redeem"[2] (e.g., Ex. 6:6; Isa. 43:1). Why would Job use such a theologically loaded word? How does his use of this term show the depth of his despair?

The "Leviathan" mentioned in verse 8 would have been familiar to ancient Israelites, even though he is strange to us. In light of other references to Leviathan (e.g., Job 41:1), it appears that this creature is perhaps a symbol for supernatural evil that resists God's rule and seeks to destroy and overwhelm the good order God has founded in creation. But why does Job refer to Leviathan? What does he hope Leviathan will do? How does this verse express the depth of Job's pain and despair?

2. Why Didn't I Die at Birth? (3:11–24)

In verses 11–16, where is the one place Job longs to be—the only imaginable place of rest and peace from his pain? Job lists kings and princes as other inhabitants of that place (vv. 14–15) and seems to imply that all of their accomplishments and wealth now mean nothing—that whatever happened during their earthly lives is now meaningless. Does that help us understand why Job might long for this place?

Although Job does not tell us, who is he probably referring to when he speaks of the "taskmaster" (v. 18)? How does this, again, hint at the depth of his despair?

In verse 23 Job says that he has been "hedged in" by God. Job clearly means this in a negative sense: the presence of this inexplicably angry, punishing God has become oppressive instead of welcome. But Job here uses a rare verb that appeared also in 1:10, where the Accuser said that God had "put a hedge" of blessing around Job and his possessions. The verb is rare enough that the echo is probably not coincidental. What might this imply about how Job is misunderstanding his position before God?

3. No Rest (3:25–26)

In verse 25 Job tells us of a fear that has now befallen him. He does not tell us what that fear is, but is there anything in chapters 1–2 suggesting that Job is afraid that he might lose God's favor?

Sometimes, long and ornate speeches in the Bible are given to us as prose, but the speeches of Job and his friends are recorded for us in intricate, sometimes difficult poetry. How does poetry communicate differently from prose? Why might it be important for us not merely to hear Job's ideas but also to experience them for ourselves by means of Job's vivid imagery?

Read through the following three sections on *Gospel Glimpses, Whole-Bible Connections*, and *Theological Soundings*. Then take time to consider the *Personal Implications* these sections may have for you.

Gospel Glimpses

A VISION OF LIFE WITHOUT THE GOSPEL. Job 3 is like a photographic negative to the many portrayals in both Testaments of life lived under the favor and grace of God. In this chapter, we hear a great saint contemplate the possibility of life without the smile of God—and his vision is dark indeed. But Job does not quite say what we would expect. Since he is at death's door and has lost every earthly blessing, it would make sense for Job to wish he were dead. But Job wishes he had never lived at all (vv. 3, 11). This shows just how much he values God and God's favor. All his life of blessing, his wonderful family, his justly deserved reputation—Job would relegate it all to deep darkness if he could not also enjoy God's favor. Just as in 1:21, it is God himself, and God's grace, that are the only things making life bearable for Job. Ironically, within the profound gloom of this chapter, we hear an echo of how deeply Job loves and values God, even though Job never names God directly in this chapter. It is important that we, who are following Job through the valley of the shadow of death, face squarely this view of life without God's grace. Doing so will only make us all the more grateful for the grace he has in fact lavished upon us.

A HARSH TASKMASTER? In a sense, Job's theology is quite robust in this chapter. But in another sense, he has completely mistaken how God is acting toward him. Job hints that God is a cruel slave master (v. 18) who hedges him in (v. 23). As a result, Job is as far away as one could be from the peace and rest that come from fellowship with God (v. 26). But although Job's mistake is understandable—he does not have the reader's perspective on the events of chapters 1–2—God is, in fact, vigorously defending Job (1:8; 2:3). Furthermore, by the end of the story Job will confess that God alone, not cosmic darkness, is his Redeemer (3:5). Profound suffering can mar and disfigure our sense of God's love, favor, and protection—but those gifts are real nonetheless.

Whole-Bible Connections

SPIRITUAL WARFARE. It is easy for Western Christians, even when theologically affirming the reality of war in "heavenly places" (Eph. 6:10–12), to deny in practice the reality of spiritual forces impinging on our daily existence. Although Job is expressing it negatively, his theology of creation in this chapter is the same as the rest of the Old Testament: there are evil forces of darkness attacking the light of God's good creation, including a fearsome supernatural monster (Job 3:8) who desires its dissolution. The book of Job broadens our perspective to see how great a struggle is being fought over the saints in heaven every day.

THE NEW CREATION. Although Job speaks of the day of his own birth in verses 3–10, he states his curse on that day in such a way that it almost seems to include all of creation. The perspective quickly widens from the light shining on the day of Job's birth to light and darkness in general. The echoes from Genesis 1 also imply that Job is calling cosmic darkness down on everything. Job is stating all of this negatively; he does not want to live in a universe without God's favor, which would remove the point of anything existing at all. But in a sense what Job wishes for will come true one day, when the world is refined with fire (2 Pet. 3:10) and a new heaven and earth will emerge (Rev. 21:1). But this reversal of fallen creation will arrive not only because of divine anger against human sin—God will make all things new precisely because of his desire to consummate his love with his bride, the church of Christ. What Job hopes for in this chapter will happen, but in a much happier way than he imagines.

Theological Soundings

WEEPING WITH THOSE WHO WEEP. It is easy, when a Christian friend is giving vent to his pain and despair in a way that borders on blasphemy, to lecture and correct him. In a similar way, it can be tempting, when talking with someone in immense pain, to be overwhelmed and try to comfort ourselves by telling the sufferer that, if only he would do something different, his pain would be reduced or disappear. But the friends who engage in this strategy (beginning in ch. 4), with a theology that seems more plausible than Job's, are rebuked by God in the end for not speaking rightly (Job 42:7). Job will, of course, recant his protest against God by the end of the book, and will worship humbly (42:1–6). But just as it is important to remember that this chapter is not the final word about God and creation, it is equally important to attend to it as one stage along the way. God will challenge some of Job's claims, but he does not scold or condemn Job for speaking thus—even though Job is wrong. Are we willing to sit in the dust with Christians who find themselves suffering in a way that is inexplicable to them? Are we willing to wait with them, until God gives them a renewed vision of creation?

IRRESISTIBLE POETRY. One way the narrator prevents us from insulating ourselves against Job's pain is through the poetry of this chapter. We are not simply informed that Job is in despair; the images and rising emotion of line upon line evoke the inner quality of his experience. The narrator apparently wants the reader to experience a little of what Job is suffering as we listen to his words. The reader, along with Job's friends, is meant to sit in the dust next to Job and grieve with him over a universe seemingly bereft of God's grace.

Personal Implications

Take time to reflect on the implications of Job 3 for your own life today. Consider what you have learned that might lead you to praise God, repent of sin, and trust in his gracious promises. Make notes below on the personal implications for your walk with the Lord of the (1) *Gospel Glimpses*, (2) *Whole-Bible Connections*, (3) *Theological Soundings*, and (4) this passage as a whole.

1. Gospel Glimpses

2. Whole-Bible Connections

3. Theological Soundings

4. Job 3

As You Finish This Unit . . .

Take a moment now to ask for the Lord's blessing and help as you continue in this study of Job. And take a moment also to look back through this unit of study, to reflect on key things that the Lord may be teaching you—and perhaps to highlight and underline these things to review again in the future.

Definitions

[1] **Chiasm** – A literary structure in which the first and last elements of a passage match each other, as do the second and the second-to-last, and so on, leaving one part or line isolated in the middle as the climactic part of the poem. Chiasms occur frequently in the OT.

[2] **Redemption** – In the context of the Bible, the act of buying back someone who has become enslaved or something that has been lost to someone else. Through his death and resurrection, Jesus purchased redemption for all believers (Col. 1:13–14).

Week 4: Round One of the Debate

Job 4:1–14:22

The Place of the Passage

One by one, Job's friends try to make good on their intention to show compassion to Job and to comfort him (Job 2:11), but they fail. Job's friends deeply believe in the principle that whatever people receive in life is a direct result of their behavior. After seeing Job's suffering, they are certain that Job must have done something to deserve such harsh treatment from God. As a result, they continually urge Job to repent of whatever sin caused this divine anger. That is the only comfort they have to give. On the other hand, because Job knows he has done nothing to merit this suffering, he will have no recourse except to question the justice of God—and to question God's character in the process. As Job protests God's unfair treatment of him, however, he will also begin to express remarkable faith in the God he is protesting. This faith will grow ever deeper as the debate continues.

The Big Picture

In these chapters, we watch as both Job and his three friends try but fail to explain why Job suffered the tragedies recounted in chapters 1–2.

Reflection and Discussion

Read through the complete passage for this study, Job 4–14. Then review the questions below concerning these two cycles of judgment and grace for the nations and write your notes on them. (For further background, see the *ESV Study Bible*, pages 878–892; available online at esv.org.)

1. Eliphaz's First Speech (chs. 4–5)

When Eliphaz claims that no innocent or upright man dies before his time (4:7), he is speaking to someone so sick as to be near death (2:5–7). What is Eliphaz implying about the cause of Job's suffering? How does he interpret Job's suffering in 5:17? What is his recommendation to Job to end this suffering? What does Eliphaz promise will happen to Job if he takes his advice (see 5:18–27)?

Remember what was said about Job in 1:1–3, the way in which God defended his servant in 1:8 and 2:3, and how Satan cannot point to any outstanding sin in Job's life. Is Eliphaz's advice helpful? Has he correctly diagnosed Job's problem?

Eliphaz lets Job in on a spiritual experience he had (4:12–21), which he thinks will shed light on Job's suffering. Although dreams are one valid means of revelation in the Old Testament, does Eliphaz's experience in verses 12–16 conform to other revelatory dreams in Scripture? Remember God's praise of "his servant" in 1:8. Is what the voice says in 4:17–18 true? Although it is not explicitly stated, whose voice might this be? How does this cause us to reevaluate Eliphaz's otherwise plausible statements?

2. Job's First Response to Eliphaz (chs. 6–7)

Job responds to Eliphaz by lamenting twice (6:1–13; 7:1–10) and by criticizing his false friends (6:14–30) and God (7:11–21). His first statement against his friends in 6:14 is very striking. How would you restate this verse? How is it possible, with the best of intentions, to fail to show kindness to someone desperately hurting?

As Job vents his grief, he says that he will never again see good (7:7), that this tragedy is irredeemable. Getting through each day is like slave labor (7:1). Even sleep grants him no relief (7:13–14). How does Job's experience of his own suffering help us make sense of the wish he expresses in 6:8–9?

Restate Job's dilemma in 7:20–21. What possibility does Job consider to explain why God has treated him this way? What two reasons does he give for rejecting this possibility?

3. Bildad's First Speech (ch. 8)

Bildad clearly and simply lays out a way for Job to be restored in 8:2–7. What is it? Is this any different from Eliphaz's guidance? Is this helpful or relevant to Job?

4. Job's First Response to Bildad (chs. 9–10)

Bildad has just asserted that God always treats people justly (8:3). Because Job is certain his suffering is unjust, he responds in 9:1–20 by imagining the only scenario in which justice could be done: if he could somehow take God to court and argue his case. But does Job expect this terrifying impossibility to play itself out (see especially vv. 3, 14, 16, 19–20)?

Job summarizes his case against God in 9:22–24. What new conclusions has Job reached about God on the basis of his experience in chapters 1–2?

In chapter 10, Job will test and reject different hypotheses to explain why God is treating him this way (see the second line of v. 2). What are they, and why does Job reject them (see vv. 4–7, 8–13, 14–17, 18–19)?

5. Zophar's First Speech (ch. 11)

What is Zophar's advice to Job in 11:13–20? Is his advice different than Eliphaz's or Bildad's? Are Zophar's claims in these verses true? Are they relevant to Job's situation?

Although this is an issue that will recur elsewhere, take a moment to summarize the theology of Job's friends. What role do grace and undeserved favor play in their understanding of one's relationship with God?

6. Job's First Response to Zophar (chs. 12–14)

Job in 12:13–25 offers a counterargument to his friends' insistence concerning God's justice. How does he extrapolate outward from his suffering to re-vision the way God governs the world?

In chapter 13, Job returns to his hypothetical court case against God, but here he imagines it differently than he did in chapter 9. Especially in 13:16–23, how does Job seem more hopeful when he contemplates such an encounter with God? What desire is growing within Job and beginning to dominate his thoughts?

Read through the following three sections on *Gospel Glimpses*, *Whole-Bible Connections*, and *Theological Soundings*. Then take time to consider the *Personal Implications* these sections may have for you.

Gospel Glimpses

GOSPEL FAILURE. Job's friends display a theology of strict merit: God dispenses suffering to sinners, but repentance qualifies you for God's mercy (contrast Rom. 5:6–8). This prevents them from considering the possibility that God might treat a sinner better than he deserves. And just as they do not have a category for grace in their relationship with God, so are they utterly ungracious with Job, telling him that all of his suffering is justly deserved (Job 8:2–3)—or maybe is even *less* than he deserves (11:6). For his part, Job hits his low point in chapters 9–10. Nowhere else will he portray God in so sinister and cruel a way; after these chapters, his hope that he might somehow be reconciled will grow ever stronger. But Job is never quite able to release his suspicions that God is a bully or a monster, until God himself speaks to him. In other words, the only "glimpses of the gospel" in the first round of the debate are negative ones. These chapters portray a failure of human graciousness in the way Job's friends speak to him, while also demonstrating Job's failure to imagine the reality of a gracious God.

Whole-Bible Connections

PRESERVATION OF THE SAINTS. Job's speech in chapter 9 is difficult to read, especially the summary of his case against God in verses 22–24. Even more distressing is Job's temptation to curse God and thus fail Satan's test in chapter 1. But there is a ray of hope. When Job portrays God as essentially a cruel dictator or bully, he is just a half-step away from cursing God and proving Satan right. But however slight the difference is between claiming that God is a tyrant and actually cursing that tyrant—Job will do the former but not the latter. Given the things Job has said about God, it is strange, of course, that he does not give up on God. Why would anyone continue in relationship with a God who seems to laugh when innocent lives are ruined (9:23)? But even when Job is saying things about God of which he will be thoroughly ashamed later (42:6), he cannot give up on God. Even when God seems to be cursing Job, Job will not curse back. Job's perseverance in faith seems inexplicable except for the fact that God will not allow his children to fall away totally from him. In the same way, when God puts us in a situation in which we might think we have every reason to give up on him, God the Spirit will enable us to endure in our relationship with him, imperfectly but sincerely: "Though he slay me, I will hope in him" (13:15).

Theological Soundings

LIMITS OF HUMAN KNOWLEDGE. In a general sense, the counsel of Job's friends is true: God never twists justice (8:3) and always receives penitents (11:13–15). In fact, Eliphaz's counsel in 5:17 sounds remarkably like Proverbs 3:11–12. But when they insist that Job must have sinned in order to be suffering God's judgment, the friends are completely wrong. Job, on the other hand, uses his tragedy from chapters 1–2 as a framework for God's action and character in a general sense, as if now he knows who God really is and how he acts toward his creation. Although Job's conclusion is the opposite of that of the friends, he is overextending himself in a similar way. As he will learn by the end of the book, he doesn't really know what he is talking about (Job 38:2–3). In presenting us with so many speakers who misunderstand their own situation and what God is doing, the book of Job is nudging us to reflect on the limits of our knowledge and on our ability to damage others by assuming that we understand their situation.

WISE AND HEALING SPEECH. Job is a part of the Bible's "wisdom literature," and thus it joins books like Proverbs and Ecclesiastes in their quest to understand the complexities of God's creation and how we can live skillfully and blessedly within that order. Wisdom literature will frequently focus on wise speech as something that provides healing to others (see Prov. 10:11, 21; 12:18; 13:14; 15:4). The book of Job seems to be exploring the same theme by giving us so many bad examples! The speeches of Job's friends are the opposite of wise speech, which brings healing and life. In fact, the speeches of the friends seem deliberately calculated to shock: although much of what they say seems sensible and can find support (in a general way) from other passages in Scripture, they make some comments along the way that are incredibly ugly. There is an implied warning in these chapters that, when we speak with people who are suffering, we can be "biblical" and plausible—and yet still deeply wound someone of whom God thinks highly.

Personal Implications

Take time to reflect on the implications of Job 4–14 for your own life today. Consider what you have learned that might lead you to praise God, repent of sin, and trust in his gracious promises. Make notes below on the personal implications for your walk with the Lord of the (1) *Gospel Glimpses*, (2) *Whole-Bible Connections*, (3) *Theological Soundings*, and (4) this passage as a whole.

1. Gospel Glimpses

2. Whole-Bible Connections

3. Theological Soundings

4. Job 4–14

Renewal - the way GOD intended life to be No death by natural causes.
No end; a brand new beginning
Turning point for Job at the end of ch 14

As You Finish This Unit . . .

Take a moment now to ask for the Lord's blessing and help as you continue in this study of Job. And take a moment also to look back through this unit of study, to reflect on some key things that the Lord may be teaching you—and perhaps to highlight and underline these things to review again in the future.

WEEK 5: ROUND TWO OF THE DEBATE

Job 15:1–21:34

The Place of the Passage

In the second round of the debate between Job and those who have come to "comfort" him, his friends deepen their hostility toward Job and their accusations of him. They continue in their unshakable certainty that he has sinned in some way and must repent. Job continues to register his protest of unjust treatment by God (and still draws inferences about God's character from this treatment), but his hope for reconciliation with the God who has caused him so much agony grows stronger and stronger, leading to beautiful statements of faith (Job 16:18–21; 19:23–27). In other words, Job imagines an encounter with God sometimes as a chance to win (impossibly) his court case against God and sometimes as an opportunity to reconcile with God. Even when Job says foolish things about God, his deepest desire is to be right with his Maker again and to reignite their relationship. Job shows a happy inconsistency in his argument, while his friends are (unfortunately) rigidly consistent in theirs.

The Big Picture

A second round of debate shows Job growing in his hope for reconciliation with God and his friends growing in their desire to condemn Job and force a confession of sin from him.

Reflection and Discussion

Read through the complete passage for this study, Job 15–21. Then review the questions below concerning this section of Job and write your notes on them. (For further background, see the *ESV Study Bible*, pages 892–902; available online at esv.org.)

1. Eliphaz's Second Speech (ch. 15)

Eliphaz makes a revealing slip in 15:4. At one level, Eliphaz is obviously worried that Job's portrayal of God as a cosmic bully (as in 12:13–25) will discourage people from fearing and trusting such a God. But what does Eliphaz seem to fear would be the case if piety had no reward? Do you think Eliphaz would have passed Satan's test?

Reflect on 15:14–16 in light of 1:1, 8. Is it true that no one can be right with God? Why might Eliphaz be so determined to portray God as displeased with *everyone*? Consider also Eliphaz's restatement of his understanding of retributive justice in 15:17–35. Is Eliphaz's description of God's moral governance realistic or plausible? Why might he be so concerned to insist that sin is always punished quickly and obviously? Why is he so intent on making Job out to be a sinner?

2. Job's Second Response to Eliphaz (chs. 16–17)

In 16:7–14, Job gives a terrifying description of what he perceives to be God's vicious assault on him. Then, in verses 15–17, he describes the tragic results of this imagined assault. By the end of the book, Job will understand that the Lord is actually a mighty warrior on his side; God is not his enemy. But this chapter represents one stage in Job's journey. It may be that, even when there is no outstanding sin in our lives, we feel we are under attack from God. Remembering that this passage is not the final word on the subject, restate, in your own words, Job's experience in these verses.

In 16:18–22, Job makes a remarkable statement of faith in a heavenly friend and advocate, even when no one else supports him (v. 20). How certain is Job of this advocate? How can you tell that it is no mere human being filling this role? How will Job benefit from his advocate's speech on his behalf?

Job began his speeches in chapter 3 by wishing he could rest in death in Sheol. By 17:10–16, however, this has changed. What is keeping Job from longing for Sheol? How does this show the change occurring in his heart?

3. Bildad's Second Speech (ch. 18)

In 18:4, Bildad implies that, when Job complains about God's injustice, Job is asking that an exception be made for him to the laws of the moral governance of the universe. What assumption is Bildad making that would cause him to misunderstand Job's speech in this way?

4. Job's Second Response to Bildad (ch. 19)

In chapter 19, Job again rebukes his friends (vv. 2–6) and complains of God's attack on him (vv. 7–12) and his resulting social isolation (vv. 13–19). But then he speaks wondrously of his Redeemer (vv. 23–27). Each verse is very significant. In verse 25, the phrase translated "stand upon the earth" is more literally "rise above the dust." Although "dust" can be a poetic way of referring to the earth (Job 5:6), it is more often in Job a way of referring to the grave (Job 7:21; 17:16; 20:11; 21:26; see also Ps. 22:15; Isa. 26:19; Dan. 12:2). If this is the correct way to read the verse, what is Job saying in his expectation that his Redeemer—who lives—will rise above or triumph over the "dust"? Remember as well that Job is terribly sick and expecting to die soon; this is why he desires that there would be a permanent record of his words (Job 19:23–24). How does this help us understand "at the last" in verse 25 and "after" in verse 26?

The reference to Job's skin (19:26) probably represents Job's whole body (see the same idea in Job 2:4; 10:11; 18:13). As a result, his skin's being "destroyed" is probably a way of speaking of death. What hope does Job have for what will happen after his physical death? How does this hope connect with the action of his Redeemer in verse 25? And what does this hope imply about any change in the relationship between Job and God?

Job gives a serious warning to his friends in the final two verses of this chapter. Is Job speaking rightly here? Can you think of other passages containing warnings about harsh, hasty, reckless, or damaging speech? How does this help us to reevaluate how we must speak to the "Jobs" we will meet in our lives?

5. Zophar's Second Speech (ch. 20)

What does Zophar speak of in this chapter? Is this different from his earlier speech in chapter 11 or from the other friends' speeches? Is there a sense in which what he says is true? Is this relevant or helpful to Job?

How many references to God can you find in Zophar's account of retribution? Go back and skim Eliphaz's and Bildad's descriptions of retribution in their second speeches (15:17–35; 18:5–21). How often do they mention God? In contrast, even when he has negative things to say, how often will Job talk of God? How does this difference reflect their differing priorities?

6. Job's Second Response to Zophar (ch. 21)

Job will spend this chapter saying the same thing from different angles. Focus on verses 7–13: in contrast to Zophar's too-tidy account of God's judgment, how does Job portray God's governance of the world? Is he right?

Read through the following three sections on *Gospel Glimpses*, *Whole-Bible Connections*, and *Theological Soundings*. Then take time to consider the *Personal Implications* these sections may have for you.

Gospel Glimpses

HOPE OF RESURRECTION. Job's brief statement of hope in a Redeemer in chapter 19 is justly famous. Although it is not exactly clear how he knows, Job is certain that he has a champion and advocate who will defend him. This is in line with the hope for a mediator that Job expresses elsewhere (9:32–33; 16:18–22), but here Job develops those thoughts by envisioning this Redeemer's triumph over the "dust," to Job's benefit. Somehow, Job's Redeemer will triumph over the powers of death and hell that now surround and overwhelm him so that, after his death, Job will be able to see God—from within his own body! This vision of God implies Job's reconciliation with God and his blessed joy in God's presence (Rev. 22:4). The frustratingly elusive God (Job 9:11) will be absent no longer.

Whole-Bible Connections

REPENTANCE AND MERIT. Although they will not quite say it this way, Job's friends appear to think of repentance as a way to gain merit with God. Just as they believe that suffering is always, only, and immediately punishment from God for sin, so also they speak of suffering as a chance to repent, reform one's life, and return in obedience to God; God then blesses the penitent person (for an early example of this, see 5:8–27). Although the New Testament will also insist on the necessity of repentance (Luke 13:3), such repentance plays a distinctly different role in how the New Testament portrays a sinner's restoration to God. There is no room in the friends' theology for love and favor from God toward the godless while they are still sinners (Rom. 4:5; 5:6–8), nor of acceptance of sinners purely on the merits of their Redeemer (Phil. 3:7–10). In contrast, the friends think of repentance as having power in itself to make a sinner acceptable to God. The friends' beliefs are a kind of dangerously false theology in which humans contribute to their salvation. This is very different from Job's view of God's blessings as gifts (Job 1:21) and (as we will see) is very different from how Job and God will relate in chapter 42.

Theological Soundings

BLAMING THE VICTIM. Job seems suspicious in 19:3–4 of his friends' insistence that he has sinned. His suspicions are justified. Why do the friends spend chapter after chapter assuring Job that he has merited God's anger, despite Job's publicly pious life (see ch. 31)? One possibility is that Job's friends are threatened by Job's suffering because, if Job really has done nothing to deserve his suffering, the same suffering might come on them. They may, in fact, be offended by that possibility: if God responds to obedience by sometimes allowing pain, is their obedience "for nothing" (remember 1:9)? As hinted at above, the friends do not give much evidence of loving God for his own sake. Nor do they give us much hope that they would have passed Satan's test. As a result, they are driven to accuse and condemn a man of whom God speaks extraordinarily highly (1:8), one with whom not even Satan can find fault.

THE SUBTLETY AND CERTAINTY OF RETRIBUTION. It is comforting to believe (as Job's friends do) that we live in a universe in which pain occurs only when it is deserved. But sometimes, when faced with the apparent randomness of suffering, we might be tempted to deny (as Job does in ch. 21) that faithfulness ever makes any practical difference in this life. The Bible clearly and frequently affirms that God rewards his children in both this life and the next, while showing much more latitude and openness to when and exactly how each individual reaps what he sows. For instance, many proverbs assure us that, contrary to Job's protest, God does uphold the moral order of his creation—but they are also noticeably vague regarding how and when that judgment will come (see, e.g., Prov. 10:24; 11:21; 12:14; 13:9). God's Word teaches us to be certain that God will render to each according to his work (Ps. 62:12) but also calls for trust as God works out his own judgment, in his own time and way.

Personal Implications

Take time to reflect on the implications of Job 15–21 for your own life today. Consider what you have learned that might lead you to praise God, repent of sin, and trust in his gracious promises. Make notes below on the personal implications for your walk with the Lord of the (1) *Gospel Glimpses*, (2) *Whole-Bible Connections*, (3) *Theological Soundings*, and (4) this passage as a whole.

1. Gospel Glimpses

2. Whole-Bible Connections

3. Theological Soundings

4. Job 15–21

As You Finish This Unit . . .

Take a moment now to ask for the Lord's blessing and help as you continue in this study of Job. And take a moment also to look back through this unit of study, to reflect on some key things that the Lord may be teaching you—and perhaps to highlight and underline these things to review again in the future.

WEEK 6: ROUND THREE OF THE DEBATE

Job 22:1–27:23

The Place of the Passage

In a way that seems designed to frustrate and tire the reader, the debate continues between Job and his friends over the reason for his suffering and the moral coherence of God's world, with none of the participants substantially changing their position. The friends continue to cling to their rigid understanding of retributive justice. Job, on the other hand, will continue to question God's justice and will express a remarkable faith that somehow he and God will be reconciled. The only new element in the debate's final round is Bildad's unusually short speech in chapter 25 and Zophar's silence. It is as if the friends run out of things to say as the book journeys closer to Job's encounter with God.

The Big Picture

The debate between Job and his friends breaks. Job and his friends have no way to resolve the problem of Job's suffering.

Reflection and Discussion

Read through Job 22–27, the focus of this week's study. Following this, review the questions below concerning this section of the book of Job and write your responses. (For further background, see the *ESV Study Bible*, pages 902–909; available online at esv.org.)

1. Eliphaz's Last Speech (ch. 22)

How is Eliphaz in verses 2–4 misunderstanding Job's claim to innocence—Job's assertion that he has done nothing to deserve what befell him in chapters 1–2? Also, has Job committed any of the sins described in 22:5–11? (Remember the narrator's evaluation of Job at the beginning of ch. 1.) Eliphaz was clearly a man who took obedience to God very seriously, thought he had a solid grasp of theology, and was a skilled poet. But how is he portrayed by the narrator? How does this portrayal prompt you to reevaluate yourself and how you might counsel someone who is suffering?

Eliphaz and his friends pressure Job to confess the sin that they think has provoked this terrible treatment from God, promising him complete restoration if he does. But if Job were to give in to them and compromise his integrity by confessing an imaginary sin in order to regain his blessed life, what implications would this have for his relationship with God, and for the secondary value of blessings in that relationship? How are the friends unintentionally advancing Satan's agenda for Job?

2. Job's Last Response to Eliphaz (chs. 23–24)

In 23:1–7, Job again expresses his desire to make his case before God (v. 4) that what happened to him in chapters 1–2 was undeserved. But Job envisions the encounter much differently than he did in 9:2–20, where he imagined that God would simply overwhelm him even though Job was right and God was wrong. How does Job express his growing hope that somehow he and God will be reconciled?

In 23:8–17, hope again sinks into gloom as Job vents his frustration over God's absence and his fear over what might yet be in store for him (see vv. 14–15). In spite of all this, however, Job holds on to his integrity before God—his innocence of any sin that might have earned his tragedy (vv. 7, 12, 17). How is it that Job's integrity, his refusal to give up on his sense of justice, drives him in basically the right direction, continuing to seek after God even when it seems hopeless or terrifying?

In 24:1–12, in what ways does Job state that mankind takes advantage of God's (apparent) slowness in judgment?

The poetry in 24:13–17 is intense and impressionistic. Sketch the shifting images of Job's poetry as he points to another example of sin that continues while God's judgment is slow to come.

3. Bildad's Last Speech (ch. 25)

Bildad is so concerned to make Job out to be a sinner that he insists no human being could ever be right with God (v. 4). Bildad further insists that even the most exalted dimensions of creation are displeasing to God (v. 5). How does this square with creation texts like Genesis 1 and Psalm 104? What reason does Bildad give in verses 5–6 for insisting that everything in creation is disgusting to God? Is this a valid inference?

4. Job's Last Response to Bildad (chs. 26–27)

Job's speech in chapter 26 is one of the most stirring in the entire book. His words seem provoked by Bildad's statement in 25:2 about God's dominion in heaven, almost as if Job is going to open Bildad's eyes to what that dominion really looks like. In the opening three verses of the chapter, how does Job fault Bildad? What must wisdom be able to do in order for it to be real?

Job describes different aspects of God's creation in 26:5–10. Old Testament descriptions of creation often emphasize the security and stability of the environment God has made for human beings. What parts of the cosmos are described in these verses, and how are the stability and goodness of God's creation emphasized?

God's battle against cosmic chaos, symbolized by the serpent, is described in verses 11–13. How is each of these verses stated in a way that highlights the certainty of God's victory? How is the serpent described in verse 13? How would this chapter have been deeply comforting to Job, who began his speeches by speaking of a more-than-natural darkness that he wished would cover the entire earth?

On what note does Job end chapter 26 (in verse 14)? What does he imply about God's greatness?

In 27:7–23, Job seems to contradict himself by speaking of the judgment of the wicked as being certain. But note verse 7: who is the most likely candidate for the role of "my enemy"? What is Job saying to his friends in this passage?

Read through the following three sections on *Gospel Glimpses*, *Whole-Bible Connections*, and *Theological Soundings*. Then take time to consider the *Personal Implications* these sections may have for you.

Gospel Glimpses

THE DANGERS OF FOOLISH SPEECH. It is impossible to read Job carefully without being sobered by our ability to damage people God loves and approves of merely by what we say. Just like Job's friends, we can sound very spiritual and give advice that is superficially plausible and theologically correct, only to malign deeply a servant of God (22:5–11) and torture him in the process (19:2). We will see how, when God finally speaks to Job (chs. 38–41), he speaks not a word of accusation, even though he could certainly have taken Job to task for the untrue things he had said! Job's words in 26:3–4 are worth reflecting on: unless we can help real people with real problems, it does not matter how correct or well-spoken we might be. Our wisdom is worthless. In sharp contrast to the "wisdom" of Job's friends, genuine wisdom does not accuse or blame by giving self-righteous advice.

Whole-Bible Connections

THE DIVINE WARRIOR. In the Old Testament, God is portrayed as both a gentle and tender shepherd (Isa. 40:11) and a mighty warrior (Ex. 15:3). The Old Testament helps us understand that supernatural forces of chaos and evil threaten the stability and safety of God's world and God's people—but God is hailed as the one who goes to war to defend us (out of many texts, see Psalms 18; 46; 74; Isa. 27:1; Hab. 3:3–15; compare Rev. 19:11–16). Job 26 joins these other texts in expanding our vision of a great battle being waged in God's world. The victory is certain, but the conflict is so great that it can be expressed only in symbolic language.

WAITING FOR DIVINE JUDGMENT. Although by the end of the book Job will realize that he is wrong to claim that God fails to execute justice in the human sphere, other biblical passages show why judgment is sometimes slow to come to fruition. James 5:7 calls for patiently waiting for the Lord's coming while suffering oppression. Paul warns us in Romans 2:4–5 that God defers judgment in kindness, which is meant to lead to repentance. He also points to the cross as the ultimate act of God's justice, as God the Son takes on himself the punishment for sins that God the Father, in his forbearance, passed over (Rom. 3:25).

Without at all agreeing with Job's protest, therefore, other passages nevertheless echo his concern for justice.

Theological Soundings

DIVINE TRANSCENDENCE. The Old Testament wonderfully affirms that God reveals himself in nature (Ps. 19:1) and in special revelation to his people (Ex. 3:6). But the Old Testament also affirms that God remains unfathomably transcendent: he dwells in deep darkness (Ps. 97:2), in an utterly different category from everything in creation (Isa. 40:18), and before him the greatest parts of creation are dust and less than nothing (Isa. 40:15). Not even Moses could have survived the sight of God's face (Ex. 33:20). Job expresses this beautifully in 26:14, describing God's victory over the twisting serpent that Isaiah and the psalmist celebrate (Isa. 51:9–11; Ps. 74:12–17) as "but the outskirts of his ways." We will spend an eternity journeying ever deeper into the infinite delightfulness of the Lord, even as he in some respects will remain infinitely above us.

Personal Implications

Take time to reflect on the implications of Job 22–27 for your own life today. Consider what you have learned that might lead you to praise God, repent of sin, and trust in his gracious promises. Make notes below on the personal implications for your walk with the Lord of the (1) *Gospel Glimpses*, (2) *Whole-Bible Connections*, (3) *Theological Soundings*, and (4) this passage as a whole.

1. Gospel Glimpses

2. Whole-Bible Connections

3. Theological Soundings

4. Job 22–27

As You Finish This Unit . . .

Take a moment now to ask for the Lord's blessing and help as you continue in this study of Job. And take a moment also to look back through this unit of study, to reflect on some key things that the Lord may be teaching you—and perhaps to highlight and underline these things to review again in the future.

WEEK 7: JOB'S FINAL SPEECH

Job 28:1–31:40

The Place of the Passage

In chapters 29–31, Job makes a final assertion of his innocence of any sin that might explain the tragedies of chapters 1–2. He invokes the strongest form of speech available to him in his culture, a self-imprecation,[1] placing himself under God's curse if he has in fact committed any of the sins he lists. In three chapters, Job moves from his blessed past (ch. 29) to his present miserable state (ch. 30) and then to a solemn assertion of his innocence (ch. 31). After this, Job has nothing left to say.

Before his final speech, however, Job delivers a poetic reflection on wisdom (ch. 28). He says that God's wisdom is paradoxically inaccessible and yet available to human beings. Wisdom involves not only skillful and insightful decision making but also insight into created reality and how God interacts with and intervenes within that reality. The question driving chapter 28, "Where can wisdom be found?," is essentially the question of the entire book. The chapter thus seems to be a sort of commentary on Job's story so far.

The Big Picture

In a final and climactic way, Job asserts his integrity before God and the undeserved nature of his suffering.

Reflection and Discussion

Read through the complete passage for this study, Job 28–31. Then review the questions below concerning this transitional section of the book of Job and write your notes on them. (For further background, see the *ESV Study Bible*, pages 909–916; available online at esv.org.)

1. Where Can Wisdom Be Found? (ch. 28)

The poem of chapter 28 advances in three distinct movements in verses 1–11, 12–19, and 20–28. What argument is this poem making about wisdom? Where is the only place that humans can access the wisdom embedded in creation? How does this poem act as a kind of implicit commentary on the failure of Job and his friends to explain his suffering?

Reflect on the final statement of the poem in verse 28. Does the fact that no one can find the wisdom present in creation except by coming before God in reverent devotion bode well or poorly for Job? Why? Does it bode well or poorly for his friends? Why?

2. Job's Final Defense (chs. 29–31)

As he remembers his past blessings, what is the first lost blessing that Job laments, in 29:2–5? How does this demonstrate his integrity and spiritual priorities?

In 29:7–10 and 21–25, Job laments the loss of his former reputation. While this may seem a trifling complaint, we learn the reason for Job's sterling reputation in verses 11–17. In what ways did Job live out his faith? How does Job lament not only for himself but for how his tragedy has affected others? How does this help to explain his pain over the damage to his reputation in 30:1–8, 9–15?

Take time to reflect on how troubling and offensive it would have been to Job to have helped so many (29:11–17) yet still to suffer what he describes in 30:16–26 (note especially vv. 25–26). Although Job's protest against God's injustice is troubling, how do passages like this help us understand why Job says these things?

Review chapter 31. How did Job live out his faith in practical ways? How did he walk closely with God and work for justice for his neighbor? What practical steps can you take today to imitate Job's faith and practice?

Reflect on Job's cry in 31:6: "Let God know my integrity!" What is Job's deepest desire, which drives all of his assertions of innocence, even when those assertions become protests against God's alleged injustice?

Read through the following three sections on *Gospel Glimpses*, *Whole-Bible Connections*, and *Theological Soundings*. Then take time to consider the *Personal Implications* these sections may have for you.

Gospel Glimpses

JOB'S LONGING TO BE RIGHT WITH GOD. Amazingly, not once in any of his speeches does Job ask for a return to the blessed life he enjoyed at the beginning of the book. As he suffers under what he (mistakenly but understandably) thinks is God's wrath, his deepest desire is to be right with God again (31:6), to experience and rest in God's friendship (29:4). Job clearly values that relationship more than he does his health, his reputation, or even his family. Even when Job rails against what he considers God's unjust treatment of him, the desire animating his protest is a good one. By the end of the book, the Lord will vindicate Job and again embrace him in friendship, the deepest blessing Job could possibly enjoy.

JESUS, THE ADVOCATE OF THE POOR. As discussed below, Job's faith expressed itself in powerful and costly good deeds. In Job's concern for the widow and orphan, he prefigures Jesus Christ, who has executed divine justice in a way Job never could have (Isa. 42:1–4), even going so far as to take the lowest place of all (Phil. 2:5–11), and becoming a beggar in order to enrich us (2 Cor. 8:9). Thus Christians, in response, are called to express the love and grace of God in Christ to the widows and orphans they encounter.

Whole-Bible Connections

THE VALUE OF A GOOD NAME. Good standing with others is not to be valued above good standing with God, and Christians are warned against expecting praise from the world (John 15:18; 1 Cor. 4:13). Yet the Old Testament wisdom literature speaks of the value of a good reputation (Prov. 22:1; Eccles. 7:1) and of the danger of hurting others through our speech (Prov. 10:18). Job's lost reputation was not his deepest pain, but it was one part of it. As we listen to Job lamenting how everyone ganged up on him in a kind of feeding frenzy (Job 30:1–15), it is appropriate to reflect on how we can defend each other through our speech, so that those imitating Job's piety and suffering like him are never defamed and abused but rather are honored.

Theological Soundings

HELPING THE ORPHAN AND WIDOW. Although Job expresses each sin in chapter 31 negatively, in the process he provides a powerful description of faith working itself out in love: Job never mistreated the people who worked for him (vv. 13–15), never mistreated the poor (vv. 16–23), and loved his enemies (vv. 29–32). This chapter stands as a permanent testimony to the kind of active faith that is sorely needed in a world in which God sometimes allows terrible suffering.

Personal Implications

Take time to reflect on the implications of Job 28–31 for your own life today. Consider what you have learned that might lead you to praise God, repent of sin, and trust in his gracious promises. Make notes below on the personal implications for your walk with the Lord of the (1) *Gospel Glimpses*, (2) *Whole-Bible Connections*, (3) *Theological Soundings*, and (4) this passage as a whole.

1. Gospel Glimpses

2. Whole-Bible Connections

3. Theological Soundings

4. Job 28–31

As You Finish This Unit . . .

Take a moment now to ask for the Lord's blessing and help as you continue in this study of Job. And take a moment also to look back through this unit of study, to reflect on some key things that the Lord may be teaching you—and perhaps to highlight and underline these things to review again in the future.

Definitions

[1] **Imprecation** – A curse that calls down God's just judgment on someone deserving of punishment. Job engages in a shortened form of a self-imprecation, which is a curse on oneself. The fuller form of this sort of imprecation can be found in passages such as Genesis 21:23 and 2 Samuel 11:11. It is tantamount to saying, "May God strike me dead if I have done this."

WEEK 8: ELIHU'S SPEECHES

Job 32:1–37:24

The Place of the Passage

The speeches of Elihu contained in these six chapters have been interpreted in two main ways throughout church history. Some have argued that the speeches contain helpful counsel that prepares Job for the even greater revelation of God in chapters 38–41, while others argue that the speeches repeat the condemnations of Job's friends and thus represent the last frustrating failure of human wisdom to help Job. The study questions for these chapters will help readers consider these alternatives and come to their own conclusions.

The Big Picture

These chapters represent one last attempt by man to resolve the problem of Job's suffering before the Lord appears.

Reflection and Discussion

Read the entire text for this week's study, Job 32–37. Then review the following questions concerning this section of Job and write your notes on them. (For further background, see the *ESV Study Bible*, pages 917–926; available online at esv.org.)

1. Elihu's Introduction (ch. 32)

We learn of Elihu's purpose in 32:14: He will provide Job a different answer than what his three friends have offered. According to verses 7–10, why has Elihu waited so long to give this new answer? Remember that in Scripture, wisdom is passed on from father to son, from the aged to the young (see, e.g., Prov. 23:22). What makes Elihu confident to do something unconventional, such as speaking in such company?

As you read chapter 32, how would you characterize Elihu? He is obviously intelligent and well-spoken, but what is implied about him through his words?

2. Elihu's Second Speech: God Is Not Silent (ch. 33)

In 33:8–13, Elihu summarizes his understanding of Job's complaint and specifies which part he will address first: the claim that God is silent. To what extent is Elihu's quotation of Job a fair summary of Job's protest against God? Is there a way in which Elihu has not listened closely to Job?

In verses 14–18, 19–22, and 23–28, Elihu lists three ways in which God speaks to man. What are they, and what (according to Elihu) is God's purpose in each? (See vv. 17, 19, 27.) Given Job's character (see 1:1–3), are Elihu's insights relevant or helpful to Job?

3. Elihu's Third Speech: Divine Justice (ch. 34)

Elihu addresses Job's complaint about divine injustice more directly in this chapter (vv. 5–6). How does Elihu defend God's justice in verses 10–12? Is this different from what Job's other friends have said (see especially 8:3)?

In verses 13–17, Elihu defends God's right to govern the world. What evidence does he enlist to show that no one can or should question God's justice? Is there anything beyond a "might-makes-right" philosophy here?

4. Elihu's Fourth Speech: God Unaffected by Sin (ch. 35)

Although Elihu's quotation of Job in 34:5–6 was accurate, is his quotation in 35:2–3 fair? How has Elihu apparently misunderstood Job's protest of God's treatment of him? Although Job accuses God of unjust treatment, would he ever say that integrity did not matter? (Remember passages like 13:16 and 23:7.)

In verses 5–8, Elihu answers his own question of verse 3. Then, in verses 9–16, Elihu provides an answer as to why God is sometimes silent and distant. What are these answers? Are they relevant or helpful to Job? How different are they from the ideas of Job's other friends? (For vv. 6–8, compare passages like 11:7–8; 22:12; 25:2–4.)

5. Elihu's Fifth and Sixth Speeches: Suffering an Opportunity to Repent (36:1–21) and God's Justice in the Storm (36:22–37:24)

Consider Elihu's account of God's ordering of the world in 36:5–12. According to Elihu, why does God exalt some (v. 7) and humble others (vv. 8–9)? Does Elihu in this speech help Job to understand his own suffering?

Elihu's final speech sets the orderly creation as parallel to divine justice—that is, just as God keeps his physical creation in good order, so also does he maintain the moral order of things. In order to make this argument, Elihu moves from rain (36:27–28) to storm and lightning (36:29–33) and thunder (37:1–5) and concludes with God's power in the storm (37:6–13). How does Elihu apply God's power in the storm to Job (36:22–24 and 37:14–20)? How does he want Job to think about or speak differently to God as a result of these truths?

Read through the following three sections on *Gospel Glimpses*, *Whole-Bible Connections*, and *Theological Soundings*. Then take time to consider the *Personal Implications* these sections may have for you.

Gospel Glimpses

THE HOPED-FOR MEDIATOR. Elihu envisions a rescuer or "mediator" (33:23) who will speak for Job, echoing Job's desire for such a figure earlier in the book (9:33; 16:18–22; 19:25–27). This mediator knows the way of righteousness (33:23) and defends in the courts of heaven the one destined for death (vv. 24–25), seeking his salvation instead. How is such rescue possible? Only by the payment of "a ransom" (v. 24). In response, the one who has suffered is reconciled to God and he shouts for joy (v. 26), acknowledging the forgiveness of his sins (v. 27). Who is this one who has "redeemed my soul from going down into the pit" (v. 28)? Elihu, surely unknowingly, is here anticipating the Son of God himself, Jesus Christ, who paid the "ransom" for sinners (Mark 10:45) to rescue them from death and hell and to bring them eternal life in the courts of heaven (Rom. 6:23), where he intercedes continually for his people (Heb. 7:25).

Whole-Bible Connections

THE LIMITATIONS OF HUMAN WISDOM. Elihu is a fine poet, who obviously cares greatly for God's honor. It is understandable that he is troubled by Job's speeches. The problem is, he cannot seem to get away from the idea that suffering comes only because of sin. As a result, he fails in his goal to answer Job's problem differently than his other friends did (Job 32:14). The speeches of Elihu seem designed to frustrate, as a new participant promises a fresh angle on the problem but then repeats what has already been said. It is difficult to see much in Elihu's speeches that would have helped Job with his problem. He outlines a glorious mediator (33:23–33) but then obscures that hope in a torrent of words. We already read in chapter 28 that no one knows where to find wisdom on his own. The book of Proverbs teaches the same truth from a happier perspective. In Proverbs 2:1–6, if the son searches for wisdom, he will find it—but only because God gives it (v. 6). In Old Testament wisdom literature and elsewhere in the Bible, insight into how creation operates and how God governs it is available only as a gift from on high (James 1:5–8; compare 1 Cor. 1:20–21). At this point in the book, Job needs to hear from the Lord. No one else can help him.

Theological Soundings

THE DANGER OF HASTY SPEECH. Even though he waits a long time, Elihu becomes so frustrated with his elders that he is unable to contain himself (Job 32:16–20). Might it not have been better for Elihu to master his desire to set everyone straight and instead wait with Job for the Lord? Our social values are, in many ways, opposite those of ancient Israel; whereas ancient Israelites valued the wisdom of old age, we valorize and romanticize youth. Although the Bible does not make all of ancient Israel's social values normative for God's people in other cultures, might not we modern North Americans perhaps benefit from learning to be silent before our elders? Is there a time for us to be silent before the wise, even if younger members of the community are convinced they best know what to do or how to speak?

Personal Implications

Take time to reflect on the implications of Job 32–37 for your own life today. Consider what you have learned that might lead you to praise God, repent of sin, and trust in his gracious promises. Make notes below on the personal implications for your walk with the Lord of the (1) *Gospel Glimpses*, (2) *Whole-Bible Connections*, (3) *Theological Soundings*, and (4) this passage as a whole.

1. Gospel Glimpses

2. Whole-Bible Connections

3. Theological Soundings

4. Job 32–37

As You Finish This Unit . . .

Take a moment now to ask for the Lord's blessing and help as you continue in this study of Job. And take a moment also to look back through this unit of study, to reflect on some key things that the Lord may be teaching you—and perhaps to highlight and underline these things to review again in the future.

Week 9: The Lord's First Speech

Job 38:1–40:5

The Place of the Passage

To our great relief, the Lord finally steps into the debate that has raged in the book of Job, answering Job in a way that both humbles and satisfies him. The Lord's first speech concerns the structure and workings of creation (Job 38:4–38) and the animals living within it (38:39–39:30). In this speech, the Lord directly answers certain claims Job has made in his protests against God. The Lord directs Job to the limitations of his own knowledge, to the great goodness of creation, and to the presence of violent elements in creation that God keeps within strict limits.

The Big Picture

The Lord responds to Job by showing that his protests have been made without sufficient knowledge of creation, in ignorance of the goodness of creation and of how God contains limited pockets of chaos within it.

Reflection and Discussion

Read through the complete text for this study, Job 38:1–40:5. Then review the questions below concerning this central text of Job and write your notes on them. (For further background, see the *ESV Study Bible*, pages 926–929; available online at esv.org.)

1. God's Initial Question (38:1–3)

God speaks to Job "out of the whirlwind." Although this Hebrew word sometimes refers to a purely natural storm (Ps. 107:25), it is often used in relation to an appearance of God in which he does battle against his enemies, protects his people, and establishes his rule (Isa. 29:6; Ezek. 1:4; Nah. 1:3; Hab. 3:14; Zech. 9:14). Since Job has been claiming that God does nothing to stop injustice and evil, how would the Lord's appearance in a storm be both encouraging and challenging to Job?

God challenges Job to prepare himself for this encounter (Job 38:3)—but does he accuse Job of any sin (as the friends did)? How does this encounter with God proceed very differently from how Job imagined it might (see 9:14–20; 13:20–28)?

2. The Architecture of Creation (38:4–38)

In verses 4–7, God describes the creation of the earth. How has Job spoken of the earth in his protest against God's supposed unjust treatment of him? (See especially chs. 3 and 9.) How is God's account of creation very different from Job's? How do these differences help to refocus Job and quell his complaint?

In verses 8–11, the Lord speaks of containing the sea. Remember that the sea is often a symbol of cosmic chaos (Job 7:12). Elsewhere in the Old Testament, we read of God's ruling over the raging sea from on high (Pss. 65:7; 89:9; 93:3–4) or setting a limit to it (Jer. 5:22). How is God's treatment of the sea described in a very different way in this passage? How is God's self-portrayal different from Job's portrayal of him? How is Job supposed to think about God differently because of these verses?

At a number of points in the book of Job, the debaters have described God's moral ordering of creation by describing some part of the natural order. God does the same in 38:12–15 as he speaks of the dawn. What moral implications does the dawn have in verses 13 and 15? What is the Lord implying about the moral component of the order of creation? How does this directly answer Job's complaint concerning injustice?

Continue reading through chapter 38. Regarding all of the questions God asks, what repeated answer is implied by each one? What are the implications of this answer?

3. The Inhabitants of Creation (38:39–39:30)

The first animals God describes are lions and ravens. Although sometimes a royal image (Gen. 49:9), lions are often portrayed in the Old Testament as fearsome and frightening predators; they symbolize the wicked in Job 4:10–11 (see also Ps. 22:13, 21). Ravens are unclean (Lev. 11:15) and are associated with other sinister animals in Isaiah 34:11. When God tells Job that only he cares for these animals, what is he implying about the complex nature of his creation, as well as his goodness toward everything he has made? How does this form an answer to Job's protest against God?

Read through the Lord's questions about the rest of the animals in this chapter. What is the implied response to each one? What is Job supposed to learn from this rhetorical exercise?

4. Job's First Response (40:4–5)

God asks Job if he will continue to find fault with the way God supervises creation. What is Job's response? How has this encounter with God proceeded differently from how Job feared it might?

Read through the following three sections on *Gospel Glimpses*, *Whole-Bible Connections*, and *Theological Soundings*. Then take time to consider the *Personal Implications* these sections may have for you.

Gospel Glimpses

GOD'S GENTLENESS WITH JOB. Job has said just about everything he could about God without cursing him—according to Job, God is an amoral tyrant who laughs at good people when their lives fall apart (9:22–24). God could have angrily rebuked Job for this, but instead he only asks whether Job really knows what he is talking about (38:2). Without issuing a single condemnation of Job, he asks a series of questions that are easy to answer, all of which direct Job's focus back to God as the only one who understands or cares for every aspect of creation. These questions are not meant to humiliate or shame Job, nor is their tone sarcastic or angry, because they all have to do with things no human being would feel ashamed of for not understanding or being able to control. This is especially clear in 38:5, where the Lord directs his pupil toward the obvious answer that only God was responsible for creation. The tone is stern but gentle. Job is not being faulted or demeaned because he was not there at the moment of creation—no human being could be blamed for such a thing. Rather, God is refocusing Job's attention onto the Lord and expanding his vision of God without condemning him.

GOD'S LIMITLESS GOODNESS. God says some things that seem shocking. The image of God putting a diaper on the sea (38:9), cuddling the raging, chaotic waters, perhaps seems absurd to those used to reading about the Lord defeating chaos in battle. But God uses this deliberately strange picture to show his profound goodness. Job has been portraying God as letting chaos run free. God responds not only by describing how he strictly limits chaos (vv. 8, 10) but also by implying that he is much kinder and gentler with creation than Job has imagined. If God cares for even his enemies this way, his goodness truly knows no bounds. And God implies that he cares for the sea even as it resists and rebels against him—this is the meaning of the final reference to the "proud waves" in verse 11 (see the same phrase in Ps. 93:4). Although the symbols used here are foreign to our culture today, consideration of these images within their original context helps to explain why Job comes to worship so reverently the God he had criticized so harshly.

Whole-Bible Connections

THE CONTINUED PRESENCE OF EVIL. The natural order of God's world reflects moral and spiritual realities. When the Lord speaks of the hawk, who lives by preying on other animals (39:29–30), or the war horse, who strains for battle (39:19–25), or the other wild animals of chapter 39, he implies that he has arranged creation in such a way that some elements of violence are a part of the natural order of things (majestic hawks in hunt), while others are a part of the brokenness of this world (horses used for warfare). Job has continually extrapolated outward from his tragedy in chapters 1–2 to make sweeping statements about creation and the sinister character of the God who sustains it. Through the symbols of these predators, God grants that there are elements of violence and evil in his world that he allows to exist, but he draws a completely different conclusion from Job's concerning his world. Out of all of the participants in this wisdom debate, God is the most enthusiastic in celebrating the goodness of creation without ignoring the elements of chaos he also sustains, whether they be natural or caused by sin. In the same way, the New Testament teaches that everything God made is good and is to be received with thanksgiving (1 Tim. 4:1–5) and that God richly provides us with everything to enjoy (1 Tim. 6:17), even amid the suffering caused by sin (2 Tim. 3:1) that befalls us prior to the redemption of all things (Rev. 21:1–4).

GOD'S JOY IN CREATION. Job began by wishing he had never been born and by calling down cosmic darkness on everything God had made (ch. 3). Although he moves past that point in the subsequent chapters, Job still cannot see any way to rejoice again (7:7). In his first speech, God gently but firmly challenges Job's despair. Although God is completely realistic about that which is sinister or violent in his world, he takes Job back to the beginning, when beings higher than Job could not contain their joy as God created the world that Job now curses (38:4–7). God does not have a single bad thing to say about the place he has made, even describing his care for the animals Job would have found most frightening. This is consistent with God's evaluation of creation in Genesis 1:31 and his joy in everything he has made in Psalm 104:31. It is human beings, from our deeply limited perspective, who see creation as dark and sinister, not God.

Theological Soundings

THE LIMITATIONS OF HUMAN KNOWLEDGE. We have seen how God has portrayed creation as entirely good without denying that it houses dangerous predators and elements of chaos (such as the sea). Running throughout this description is a challenge to Job's certainty of his own conclusions. Job was not there when God put the world together (38:4–7), so how much do his conclusions count? If it were up to Job, mountain goats would cease to exist as a species (39:1–4). Deep pain is so intense an experience that it is easy for it to color everything we see, as we become as certain of our perspective as we are of our pain. But the book of Job shows us that the one person who knows the most about creation is also the most enthusiastic about it. In so doing, the book casts doubt on our dark thoughts of God and of his world that we often harbor when we suffer.

Personal Implications

Take time to reflect on the implications of Job 38:1–40:5 for your own life today. Consider what you have learned that might lead you to praise God, repent of sin, and trust in his gracious promises. Make notes below on the personal implications for your walk with the Lord of the (1) *Gospel Glimpses*, (2) *Whole-Bible Connections*, (3) *Theological Soundings*, and (4) this passage as a whole.

1. Gospel Glimpses

2. Whole-Bible Connections

3. Theological Soundings

4. Job 38:1–40:5

As You Finish This Unit . . .

Take a moment now to ask for the Lord's blessing and help as you continue in this study of Job. And take a moment also to look back through this unit of study, to reflect on some key things that the Lord may be teaching you—and perhaps to highlight and underline these things to review again in the future.

Week 10: The Lord's Second Speech

Job 40:6–41:34

The Place of the Passage

God's first speech directly answered some aspects of Job's protest against injustice, and Job has formally withdrawn his complaint (Job 40:1–5). But that first speech was not a complete answer. When one has dead children, how satisfying is it to hear about the good ordering of (for instance) different animal species? God redresses this deficit in a second speech, which directly focuses on Job's criticisms of God (40:8). He directs Job's gaze not to the natural order of things but to two terrifying beasts that represent spiritual evil. In speaking this way, he defends his justice to Job in such a way that Job is reduced to humble worship (42:1–6).

The Big Picture

The focus turns from the natural to the supernatural as God defends his justice by describing the coming battle with two fearsome monsters, Behemoth and Leviathan.

Reflection and Discussion

Read through the complete passage for this study, Job 40:6–41:34. Then review the questions below on this section of Job's prophecy and record your notes and reflections. (For further background, see the *ESV Study Bible*, pages 929–932; available online at esv.org.)

1. The Preparation of the Divine Warrior (40:9–14)

It is not uncommon in the Psalms to show the Lord radiating a luminous splendor before going to battle against his enemies (compare Pss. 29:2; 93:1; 96:6; 104:1). After *this* preparation (Job 40:9–11), what does God do in verses 12–14? How do these verses directly answer Job's complaint about divine injustice?

How do you think Job would have felt after hearing this self-description from the divine warrior? How do you think the reader is supposed to reimagine God while reading this, especially after the false descriptions of God given by Job and his friends earlier in the book?

2. Behemoth (40:15–24) and Leviathan (41:1–34)

Through the poetry of these verses, God paints Job a vivid picture of the untamable, lurking strength of Behemoth and the invincible, impenetrable fierceness of Leviathan. While God could be describing two entirely ordinary animals in these chapters, the fact that Job responds so differently to this speech compared to God's previous speech, in which he described many animals (ch. 39), makes this unlikely. Leviathan is described elsewhere as a supernatural opponent of God (Ps. 74:12–14; Isa. 27:1; Rev. 12:7–9). List some of the ways that these speeches challenge Job's claims in his speeches, expand his vision, and change his view of God.

How does God's speech about Behemoth and Leviathan challenge the theology of Job's friends?

In two places, God speaks of a coming battle with these beasts (40:19 and 41:7–8). How would this have been a comfort and a joy to Job?

What tone pervades these chapters? How would you characterize God's attitude toward these creatures, and the coming battle?

Read through the following three sections on *Gospel Glimpses*, *Whole-Bible Connections*, and *Theological Soundings*. Then take time to consider the *Personal Implications* these sections may have for you.

Gospel Glimpses

THE JOY OF THE DIVINE WARRIOR. In his descriptions of Behemoth and Leviathan, God expands Job's vision to show him a cosmic evil at loose in creation, which God will one day defeat. As he shows Job evil on a scope Job can barely comprehend, God is neither apologetic nor defensive. If anything, he seems to praise his opponents (see especially 41:12). This does not imply that there is anything good about these monsters. Rather, it shows the joyful confidence of God as he looks forward to the day when he will scour every last bit of evil from his creation and make it new. The one person who most clearly sees all that is wrong with his creation is also the one most enthusiastic about it—God. Job accepts God's perspective on his still-unredeemed world and rejoices with him. Following Job, we can withstand suffering without blackening God's character or disparaging the goodness of created life, especially as we more fully understand the great price God paid to defeat the evil at loose in his creation—by taking it upon himself at the cross in the person of Jesus.

Whole-Bible Connections

WAR IN HEAVEN. Throughout his speeches, Job has viciously criticized what he considers to be God's unjust administration of the cosmos. Although Job is aware of Leviathan (3:8), it does not occur to him that anyone other than God would be attacking him. God responds by expanding Job's vision to include a cosmic enemy who would utterly overwhelm Job, but whom God will one day defeat (41:1–8). Job is to draw several conclusions from this. First, God is not Job's enemy, as Job thought—Leviathan is, while God is Job's defender! God is also implying that he understands how much Job has suffered (in fact, he understands the true scope of Job's suffering better than Job does). But perhaps most important is the revelation that a great war is being fought behind the theater of earthly life—and we are the prize. In the crucible of inexplicable pain, a great spiritual struggle is being waged over the saints. Thankfully, God has already assured us of the outcome—defeat of our enemies and an eternity in his presence in the new heavens and the new earth.

GOD'S HIDDEN WISDOM. Our answers to evil and suffering tend to focus on trusting God in dark times, on waiting for our lives to get better, on God's working all things out for good, and on the hope of heaven. These answers are certainly not wrong. God's answer to Job, however, is entirely different: he affirms the utter goodness of the world Job has been criticizing *prior to* the redemption of all things, a world in which chaos and evil are still given some room in God's plans. While he promises to defeat this evil one day, God also sustains creation each day in the here-and-now. Trusting in God's final defeat of evil, and remaining mindful of the war being fought over us, gives us strength to endure in our relationship with God while he allows Leviathan some measure of power over us.

Theological Soundings

DEEP SYMBOLISM. Some images in the Bible are relatively easy to understand, such as when the wicked are described as lions (Job 4:10). But there is a deeper and subtler symbolism in the Bible, which is found first in the serpent of Genesis 3, a creature clearly classified as a common animal (3:1) but who also knows things only God knows (compare Gen. 3:5 with Gen. 3:22). Behemoth and Leviathan belong in this deeper category of symbolism, which speaks of realities that do not easily translate into earthly concepts or language. Their detailed physical descriptions are meant to evoke deeper spiritual realities of which we are only dimly aware. This is not the only way in which the Bible communicates, but it is one important part of God's Word to us.

Personal Implications

Take time to reflect on the implications of Job 40:6–41:34 for your own life today. Consider what you have learned that might lead you to praise God, repent of sin, and trust in his gracious promises. Make notes below on the personal implications for your walk with the Lord of the (1) *Gospel Glimpses*, (2) *Whole-Bible Connections*, (3) *Theological Soundings*, and (4) this passage as a whole.

1. Gospel Glimpses

2. Whole-Bible Connections

3. Theological Soundings

4. Job 40:6–41:34

As You Finish This Unit . . .

Take a moment now to ask for the Lord's blessing and help as you continue in this study of Job. And take a moment also to look back through this unit of study, to reflect on some key things that the Lord may be teaching you—and perhaps to highlight and underline these things to review again in the future.

Week 11: Job's Restoration

Job 42:1–17

The Place of the Passage

Job has just had his eyes opened to a coming battle with a supernatural evil he can barely imagine. In contrast to his first reply (Job 40:3–5), Job is now reduced to self-loathing because of his criticism of his Savior, and he is entirely reconciled to God's manner of administering creation before the redemption of all things (42:6). Further, Job is vindicated before his friends for his imperfect but genuine faith in God amid his crisis (vv. 7–9). Since Job has responded in faith and worship to God's speeches, and has proved beyond any doubt that he loves and is loyal to God only for God's sake (1:9), God restores Job to fullness of life and family. Job's trial was unimaginably painful, but his life ends full of blessing (42:10–17).

The Big Picture

Job is restored spiritually by being reconciled to the Lord he formerly criticized (42:1–6) and is restored socially by being vindicated before his friends (vv. 7–9) and by enjoying great blessings of prosperity and family (vv. 10–17).

Reflection and Discussion

Read through Job 42:1–17, the passage for this week's study. Then review the following questions, taking notes on the final section of Job's prophecy. (For further background, see the *ESV Study Bible*, pages 932–933; available online at esv.org.)

1. Job's Spiritual Restoration (42:1–6)

Job says he now knows that no purpose of God's can be thwarted (v. 2). Coming so soon after the description of Leviathan's defeat, this is more than a general statement of omnipotence. How would God's invincible purposes have been an immense comfort to a man who had lost so much?

The verb translated "repent" in verse 6 could also be translated "am comforted" (see ESV note). Trace the ways that either translation could be appropriate—that is, the reasons Job could be expressing either his repentance of his protest or his deep comfort with God and God's world.

"I had heard of you by the hearing of the ear, but now my eye sees you" (v. 5). What new insights has Job gained into God's character and action, and how have these insights deepened his former knowledge of God?

2. Job's Vindication before His Friends (42:7–9)

After the protests of Job's speeches, it is surprising to see God say that Job has spoken rightly (v. 7). Although this cannot be a wholesale approval of everything Job has said, how has Job shown a faith in God more genuine than that of the friends, even though the friends' theology might have been superficially more plausible?

When God commands the friends to sacrifice, and Job to pray for them so that they can be restored to God's favor (vv. 8–9), how is God contradicting the friends' theology? (How did the friends think one gained favor with God?) How would this have been a blessing to Job as well? What understandable but inappropriate attitudes toward his friends might this command have prevented Job from developing?

3. Job's Restoration in His Family (42:10–17)

In the final passage of the book, we have a sense that the nightmare is over, that Job has passed the test and Satan has withdrawn his objection to Job's faith. List the ways in which God, having restored his servant to himself, restores to Job the blessings he had lost.

Job's family and other friends come to comfort Job (v. 11)—succeeding where his three friends had failed. Strikingly, no speech is recorded; rather, concrete actions are detailed. What do Job's family and other friends do for him? Why would this have been more comforting than were all the speeches of his friends?

Read through the following three sections on *Gospel Glimpses*, *Whole-Bible Connections*, and *Theological Soundings*. Then take time to consider the *Personal Implications* these sections may have for you.

Gospel Glimpses

JOB'S FAITH. When God gave Job a close-up tour of the terrifying monster Job knows by name and reputation only, Job could have renewed his protest by claiming it was unjust of God to allow this great evil to continue to exist. Instead, Job does the opposite: he worships, entirely reconciled to God's decision to allow this evil some limited agency for a set time. He is "comforted" (v. 11) even though Leviathan is undefeated. In honoring God's decision to administer creation in this particular way, Job is able to enter into trusting fellowship with God in a way he never could before. His final speech shows him overwhelmed with his unstoppable Savior, who is at work to heal and save and restore in ways too profound for Job to understand (vv. 2–3). Job relates to God on the basis of faith and is treated by God better than he deserves as God restores him to happy fellowship with his Savior.

A RIGHTEOUS MAN INTERCEDES FOR HIS TORTURERS. God's command to Job to pray for his tormentors displays God's grace in a number of ways. First, although God is angry with Job's friends for their attack on Job, he takes the initiative to restore them to divine favor. Second, God breaks the friends' theology of currying favor with God through religious self-improvement by commanding the sacrifice of a substitute and by making them depend on the intercessory prayer of a man they thought to be beneath themselves. As Job prays for his friends, he prefigures a greater righteous man who intercedes on behalf of his torturers as one part of the grace of God to restore sinners to himself, despite their unworthiness. That man was Jesus, who on the cross prayed for the forgiveness of those who would torture and execute him (Luke 23:34).

Whole-Bible Connections

RESTORATION, RETRIBUTION, AND RESURRECTION. The book of Job nuances the biblical idea that everyone reaps what they sow. The last chapter shows God's desire to bless his children not just with knowledge of himself (42:3) but in every other good thing as well. Although God must sometimes interrupt his normal policy of blessing in order to test the reality of man's relationship with him, these interruptions are always temporary. Within the framework of the old covenant, these blessings took on a material and earthly form only, but Job's blessings anticipate those greater blessings in the new covenant, which will be seen most fully in the life of the world to come, where, "all safe and blessed, we shall meet at last." This is God's will for his children, to give us all he can, resolving tremendous pain into peace and blessing.

Theological Soundings

NOW MY EYE SEES YOU. In 42:5, Job compares all of his former knowledge of God to mere rumor and hearsay. Since Job was already a mature saint, this is quite a thing to say! But Job is entirely caught up in his vision of his victorious Savior. This is not only because God has made himself visible to Job. In his worship, Job has accepted and even come to rejoice in God's manner of ruling creation without demanding an explanation from God as to why he allowed Job's particular tragedy. Job accepts God's promise that he will one day defeat this evil even as he keeps it within bounds now. As Job does so, he is able to see God as the Sovereign Lord and not just as a business partner with whom he negotiates for a blessed life. The same is true for us: as we accept the Lord's control over evil and his eventual defeat of it, we see him as God and Lord in a new way. We are delivered from reducing him to a local, pet deity who serves our own interests. Along with Job, we say, "Now my eye sees you."

GOD'S VINDICATION OF HIS SERVANTS. When God allows Job-like suffering in our life for a certain time—suffering that is inexplicable and seemingly useless—it is possible that other Christians, with the best of intentions, will try to help us in ways that only increase our pain, as Job's friends did. It is also likely that we will say some foolish things about God that will shame us when he restores and comforts us. The book of Job teaches that God is surprisingly gentle with us as we struggle in our faith, and he vindicates those who persevere in keeping faith with God (however imperfectly) over against others who attack, lecture, or criticize his servants. This vindication is entirely on terms of grace, not merit, and is meant not to destroy Job's would-be comforters but to restore them as well. It is encouraging to remember that God cares for our relationships with other Christians and that it matters to him enough to intervene when we are humiliated and attacked without good reason.

Personal Implications

Take time to reflect on the implications of Job 42:1–17 for your own life today. Consider what you have learned that might lead you to praise God, repent of sin, and trust in his gracious promises. Make notes below on the personal implications for your walk with the Lord of the (1) *Gospel Glimpses*, (2) *Whole-Bible Connections*, (3) *Theological Soundings*, and (4) this passage as a whole.

1. Gospel Glimpses

2. Whole-Bible Connections

3. Theological Soundings

4. Job 42:1–17

As You Finish This Unit . . .

Take a moment now to ask for the Lord's blessing and help as you continue in this study of Job. And take a moment also to look back through this unit of study, to reflect on some key things that the Lord may be teaching you—and perhaps to highlight and underline these things to review again in the future.

Week 12: Summary and Conclusion

We will conclude our study of Job by summarizing the big picture of God's message through Job as a whole. Then we will consider several questions in order to reflect on various Gospel Glimpses, Whole Bible Connections, and Theological Soundings throughout the entire book.

The Big Picture of Job

The book of Job explores why God sometimes allows tremendous suffering by those who deserve it least. God seeks to give us knowledge of himself and to add to that chief blessing many other temporary ones. But Job teaches us that sometimes God must interrupt his normal policy in order to deliver us from trivializing him as a business partner or loving his gifts more than we love him as the giver. When God allows inexplicable suffering, when God gives us seemingly strong reasons to give up on him, when he appears to treat us like an enemy, he is forcing us into a relationship with him in which he is truly seen to be God and Lord—the only kind of relationship that will save us.

The book of Job shows us that, much to our surprise, a great war is being fought in heaven over the saints during such trials. We watch as Job struggles and criticizes God but cannot bring himself to give up on him, and he is vindicated for his faith. We also watch as Job's friends attempt to comfort him but only add to his pain. And we learn that the only answer in Job-like suffering, the only thing that can comfort us in inexplicable loss, is not further explanation but a deeper vision of God—especially a vision of the divine warrior going to battle for us against an enemy greater than we can imagine. Finally, we learn that these experiences are blessedly temporary and that, having confirmed us in our relationship with him, God never fails to give us exactly what we need.

Gospel Glimpses

How has Job brought new clarity to your understanding of what faith in God looks like and of how God's grace operates toward those who trust him?

Are there any particular passages or themes in Job that have led you to a deeper understanding of who Jesus Christ is and how he acts as a powerful Savior for you?

Whole-Bible Connections

How has this study of Job filled out your understanding of the biblical storyline of redemption?

Are there any themes emphasized in Job that help you to deepen your grasp of the Bible's unity?

What connections between Job and the New Testament were new to you?

Theological Soundings

Job is a very difficult book, but it speaks volumes to disciples of Christ. Has your theology shifted in minor or major ways during the course of studying Job? How so?

How has your understanding of the nature and character of God been deepened throughout this study?

Personal Implications

God wrote the book of Job to transform us. As you reflect on Job as a whole, what implications do you see for your life?

What implications for life flow from your reflections on the questions already asked in this week's study concerning Gospel Glimpses, Whole-Bible Connections, and Theological Soundings?

What have you learned in Job that might lead you to praise God, turn away from sin, or trust more firmly in his promises?

As You Finish Studying Job . . .

We rejoice with you as you finish studying the book of Job! May this study become part of your Christian walk of faith, day-by-day and week-by-week throughout all your life. Now we would greatly encourage you to study the Word of God on a week-by-week basis. To continue your study of the Bible, we would encourage you to consider other books in the *Knowing the Bible* series, and to visit www.knowingthebibleseries.org.

Lastly, take a moment to look back through this study. Review the notes that you have written, and the things that you have highlighted or underlined. Reflect again on the key themes that the Lord has been teaching you about himself and about his Word. May these things become a treasure for you throughout your life—this we pray in the name of the Father, and the Son, and the Holy Spirit. Amen.